MILITARY VEHICLES

PALADINS

BY JOHN HAMILTON

VISIT US AT
WWW.ABDOPUBLISHING.COM

Published by ABDO Publishing Company, 8000 West 78th Street, Suite 310, Edina, MN 55439. Copyright ©2012 by Abdo Consulting Group, Inc. International copyrights reserved in all countries. No part of this book may be reproduced in any form without written permission from the publisher. A&D Xtreme™ is a trademark and logo of ABDO Publishing Company.

Printed in the United States of America, North Mankato, Minnesota.
062011
092011

Editor: Sue Hamilton
Graphic Design: Sue Hamilton
Cover Design: John Hamilton
Cover Photo: U.S. Army
Interior Photos: AP-pg 15; BAE Systems-pgs 28-29; Department of Defense-pgs 8 (insert), 12-13, 22-25; Defense Video & Imagery Distribution System-pgs 1-11, 16-21, 26-27, 30-32; United States Army-pgs 14, 21 (insert) & 23 (insert).

Library of Congress Cataloging-in-Publication Data

Hamilton, John, 1959-
  Paladins / John Hamilton.
      p. cm. -- (Military vehicles)
  Includes index.
  Audience: Ages 8-15.
  ISBN 978-1-61783-077-8
  1. M109 Paladin (Howitzer)--Juvenile literature. I. Title.
  UF652.H36 2012
  623.7'475--dc23
                    2011020652

TABLE OF CONTENTS

THE M109A6 PALADIN

The United States Army's M109A6 Paladin howitzer is a technologically advanced self-propelled artillery system. It looks like a tank, but it has a larger cannon and thinner armor. Its job is to support tanks and infantry on the battlefield. It does this by firing devastating explosives from long distances.

XTREME FACT

A Paladin is a knight or heroic champion who defends the weak, or a worthy cause.

The M109A6 Paladin is an indirect fire support weapon. Groups of six Paladins usually travel several miles behind advancing forces of tanks and infantry. When heavy resistance is encountered, Paladins are given the precise location of the enemy. Paladins can rain down a tremendous amount of explosive firepower from as far away as 18.6 miles (30 km). Paladins can also fire directly at enemy units in their line of sight.

Soldiers fire Paladins at a site in Iraq.

While powerful, an M198 howitzer must be towed by another vehicle.

Paladins are large pieces of artillery called howitzers. Their explosive shells travel in a long, high arc. Most howitzers, such as the Army's M198, must be towed behind other vehicles. Paladins are self-propelled howitzers. They are tracked vehicles, like tanks, and do not need to be towed. Paladins are basically large cannons with their own built-in transportation system.

XTREME FACT

Paladins sometimes fire illumination rounds, which are parachuted flares that light up an area at night.

M109A6 PALADIN FAST FACTS

M109A6 Paladin Specifications

Length:	32.2 feet (9.8 m)
Width:	10.3 feet (3.1 m)
Height:	10.6 feet (3.2 m)
Weight (combat loaded):	31.8 tons (28.8 metric tons)
Top Speed:	38 miles per hour (61 kph)
Cruising Range:	186 miles (299 km)
Crew:	4
Main Weapon:	155mm cannon
Weapon Range:	18.6 miles (30 km)
Manufacturer:	BAE Systems

PALADIN HISTORY

The U.S. Army's M109 self-propelled howitzers went into service in 1963. They first saw combat during the Vietnam War. Since that time, the howitzers have been used in several wars, including the invasion of Iraq from 2003-2011.

An M109 self-propelled howitzer moves down a desert road in 1988 at Fort Irwin in California.

VERSIONS

Over the years, the M109 system has been continually upgraded and improved. The current version is the M109A6, which is named "Paladin." It entered Army service in 1991. The Paladin's biggest improvements include better armor, upgraded engine and suspension, and fire-control computers and navigation systems. Advanced electronics and communications allow Paladins to halt movement and fire at targets in less than one minute.

A soldier prepares the fire-control computer in an M109A6 Paladin.

More than 35 nations have bought M109 self-propelled howitzers from the United States. They include Israel, Great Britain, Saudi Arabia, South Korea, and Taiwan (shown here).

CREW

M109A6 Paladins have a crew of four soldiers. They include a commander, a driver, a gunner, and an ammunition loader. Older models of the M109 required a crew of six, which included two ammunition loaders and an assistant gunner. Advanced fire control systems added to the Paladin eliminated these two extra crew members.

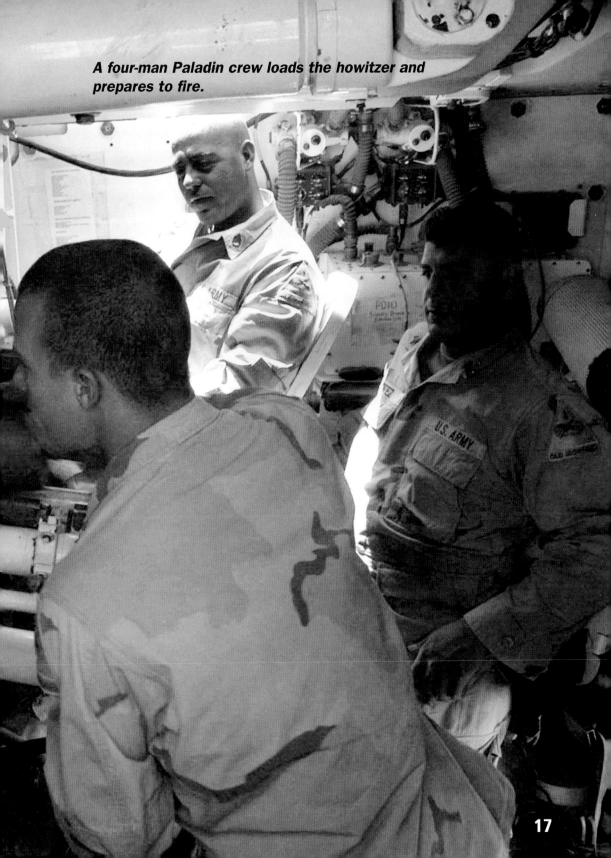

A four-man Paladin crew loads the howitzer and prepares to fire.

CANNON

The Paladin's main weapon is the M284 155mm howitzer. This cannon can fire up to four rounds per minute. The crew receives information about enemy targets on secure digital communication links. Electronic control systems compute firing data and aim the cannon. Paladins can hit targets up to 18.6 miles (30 km) away.

Driver Hatch

XTREME FACT

After firing, the Paladin's crew can move the vehicle in less than a minute, which avoids enemy counterbattery fire. This is called "shoot and scoot."

AMMUNITION

The M109A6 Paladin can stow up to 39 rounds of 155mm high-explosive shells. Each standard 155mm projectile weighs 98 pounds (44 kg). Paladins can also fire rounds that create smoke, or light up the battlefield at night.

A crewmember restocks a Paladin's ammo supply.

Soldiers test a special propellant that pushes Excalibur shells out of the barrel of the Paladin howitzers.

Excalibur shell

Some Paladins now use the Army's new M982 Excalibur shell. The 155mm Excalibur performs much like a "smart bomb" fired from an aircraft. It uses an electronic GPS guidance system and retractable fins to accurately glide to its target. The Excalibur has a range of about 25 miles (40 km).

OTHER WEAPONS

In addition to the 155mm howitzer,
the Paladin is also armed with a
.50-caliber M2 machine gun, which is
mounted on the roof of the turret. This
can be used if enemy forces somehow
get close to the Paladin, or if it is traveling
through a hostile urban area. Some Paladins
are outfitted with 40mm automatic grenade
launchers instead of machine guns.

M2 Machine Gun

ARMOR

The Paladin's chassis and turret are made of thick welded aluminum armor. In addition, the turret is lined with Kevlar, the same ballistic fabric material used in bulletproof vests. This combination protects the crew from small-arms fire and shrapnel from bombs that explode nearby.

The Paladin's crew compartment is pressurized, which shelters the crew from nuclear, biological, and chemical threats. The military calls this NBC protection.

ENGINE

The Paladin's 440-horsepower engine drives the wheel and track system, plus it powers the vehicle's electrical generator.

The M109A6 Paladin is powered by a Detroit Diesel 8V71T eight-cylinder turbocharged diesel engine.

The engine gives the Paladin a top road speed of 38 miles per hour (61.1 kph).

The Paladin's engine sits behind this panel.

XTREME FACT

Each of the Paladin's tracks has 79 links with hard rubber pads that are 17 inches (43 cm) wide. The part of the track that contacts the ground is 13 feet (4 m) long.

THE FUTURE

The U.S. Army will soon upgrade 600 of its fleet of about 975 M109A6 Paladins. The new version is called the M109 Paladin Integrated Management (PIM) vehicle.

The PIM is a major upgrade, with a new chassis, improved engine, better ammunition handling, and state-of-the-art electronics. With these improvements, the Army will rely on the Paladin for many years to come.

GLOSSARY

AMMUNITION

The bullets and shells used in weapons.

ARMOR

A strong, protective covering made to protect military vehicles.

ARTILLERY

Guns used in warfare that have a large caliber. Caliber is the diameter of a round of ammunition, measured in inches or millimeters. Artillery is usually used behind the main lines of battle to launch explosives at the enemy from a long distance. The M109A6 Paladin launches a high-explosive shell that has a caliber of 155mm (6.1 in).

COUNTERBATTERY

Modern radar systems can detect the location of incoming artillery fire. This allows enemy artillery to be attacked and hopefully destroyed.

DIESEL

A thick petroleum product that is used in diesel engines, such as those found in heavy tanks or trucks.

GLOBAL POSITIONING SYSTEM (GPS)

A system of orbiting satellites that transmits information to GPS receivers on Earth. Using information from the satellites, receivers can calculate location, speed, and direction with great accuracy.

GRENADE
A bomb with a delayed explosion thrown by hand or shot from a rifle or launcher.

HOWITZER
An artillery piece that fires relatively slow-moving shells in high arcs toward the target.

INFANTRY
Soldiers who move and fight on foot.

KEVLAR
A light and very strong man-made fiber. It is used to make helmets, vests, and other protective gear for military and law enforcement personnel.

TURRET
The low, flat armored area on the top part of a tank, which houses the main cannon and other weapons. The turret rotates, allowing a gunner to aim and fire in any direction.

VIETNAM WAR
A conflict between the countries of North and South Vietnam from 1955 to 1975. Communist North Vietnam was supported by China and the Soviet Union. The United States entered the war on the side of South Vietnam.

INDEX